The Song of Light

Written & illustrated by
T. A. Taylor

I0111003

Shannon Pot Books

© T. A. Taylor 2014

The catalogue record for this book is available
from the British Library.

ISBN 978-0-9927660-0-9

All rights reserved. No part of this publication may be reproduced, stored in or
introduced into a retrieval system, or transmitted, in any form or by any means
(electronic, mechanical, photocopying, recording or otherwise), without prior written
permission of both the copyright owner and publisher of this book.

Published by:
Shannon Pot Books
Address: Drumkeeran, Co. Leitrim. Republic of Ireland
www.shannonpotbooks.org

Designed and typeset by:
Tiger Print, 3 Knappagh Road, Sligo. Republic of Ireland

Typeset in Cambo and Devroye.

Previous page illustration:
Mammoth ivory carving,
22,000BC Grotte du pape, Brassempouy, France

This book is dedicated to

Abigail

ABOUT SHANNON POT BOOKS

Shannon Pot Books is a family-based, independent group that aims to produce writing that meets the global need and interest in sacred knowledge. Our mission is to contribute to a body of shared human understanding, and to bring forward information and ideas that can contribute in the efforts to build harmonious and peaceful societies.

Our current titles come out of this concept, and are designed to bring together knowledge held within the Native American wisdom teachings, and those that have originated in the ancient heritage of the Irish and other Celtic traditions.

OTHER TITLES
(available via Amazon retail and other outlets)

Song of the Blue Star
by B. A. Boland
236 pages, 2014. ISBN 13 978-0-9927660-2-3

For forthcoming titles please check our web site:
www.shannonpotbooks.org

The Twenty Count
written and illustrated by T. A. Taylor
ISBN 978-0-9927066-4-7 (publication date 2016)

ABOUT THE AUTHOR

T. A. Taylor is an artist living and working in Ireland.

Contents

Introduction

The ten wheels of light or energy centres situated in and around the human body contain the many circles of teaching known by the first people since the earliest times and show the inter-connectedness of our own lives with all other life on Earth. In the Native American tradition this body of knowledge is called the Sweet Medicine teaching and is taught to every child.

In this book I have joined the Celtic tradition and imagery with the Native American understanding of our world, with particular reference to the Gundestrup cauldron, a silver-plated copper bowl discovered in a peat bog in Denmark. This sacred cauldron, dated from about the first or second century B.C. is beautifully decorated on the inside and outside with many images of unidentified deities and mythological scenes, and I believe it holds a key to the ancient Celtic landscape of understanding. Other images used in the book are taken from the fragmented remains of those times when the Celtic peoples were to be found across Europe as far as the Balkans, into Greece and Asia Minor, arriving in Ireland at least three centuries B.C., until the coming of the Vikings in the ninth century A.D. The stone from the pre-history of Ireland with the megalithic sites of Newgrange and Knowth (Brúigh na Bóinne), showing detailed carving from the most ancient of times have also been absorbed into the iconography used in the book. The first peoples of Ireland can be very closely identified with the first peoples of the Americas.

In writing this book an attempt has been made to undertake the 'rosc', a form of poetry sung aloud that ignites recognition and understanding in the mind. The repetition and building of a picture scene in 'rosc' becomes an incantation that can be used as a meditation for the wheels of light.

I would like to acknowledge and thank my teachers, Mr Stennett-Wilson, Arwyn Dreamwalker, and Venerable Panchen Otrul Rinpoche, who have helped me so much on my life journey, and Warwick Hutton who was the Head of Art at Cambridge College of Art (now Ruskin University). I am also indebted to the many scholars of Irish antiquity and the sacred lineage holders of Native American wisdom and tradition.

Invocation

The Sons of Míl arrived in Ireland on the feast day of Beltene two thousand years ago, and as the poet Amairgen (Amhairghin) set his right foot upon the land he sang this poem:

'I am an estuary into the sea

I am a wave of the ocean,

I am the sound of the sea,

I am a powerful ox,

I am a hawk on a cliff,

I am a dewdrop in the sun,

I am a plant of beauty,

I am a boar for valour,

I am a salmon in a pool,

I am a lake on a plain,

I am the strength of art'

Cernunnos, the antlered deity of the Celtic peoples. The god holds a torc in one hand and a horned snake in the other.
Gilt-silver plate of the Gundestrup cauldron in Nationalmuseet, Copenhagen.

The Elements

The Native American Sweet Medicine teachings are based on the circle, beginning with the circle of elements, and grounded in the four directions.

In the centre of the circle of elements is aether. The centre is the void from which all is conceived and formed. It contains the patterns and imprints of all time, the ebb and flow of all possibilities, the song of creation and is the balanced central axis of all the elements that are formed between the sun and the earth, holding the female and male energies in perfect resonance.

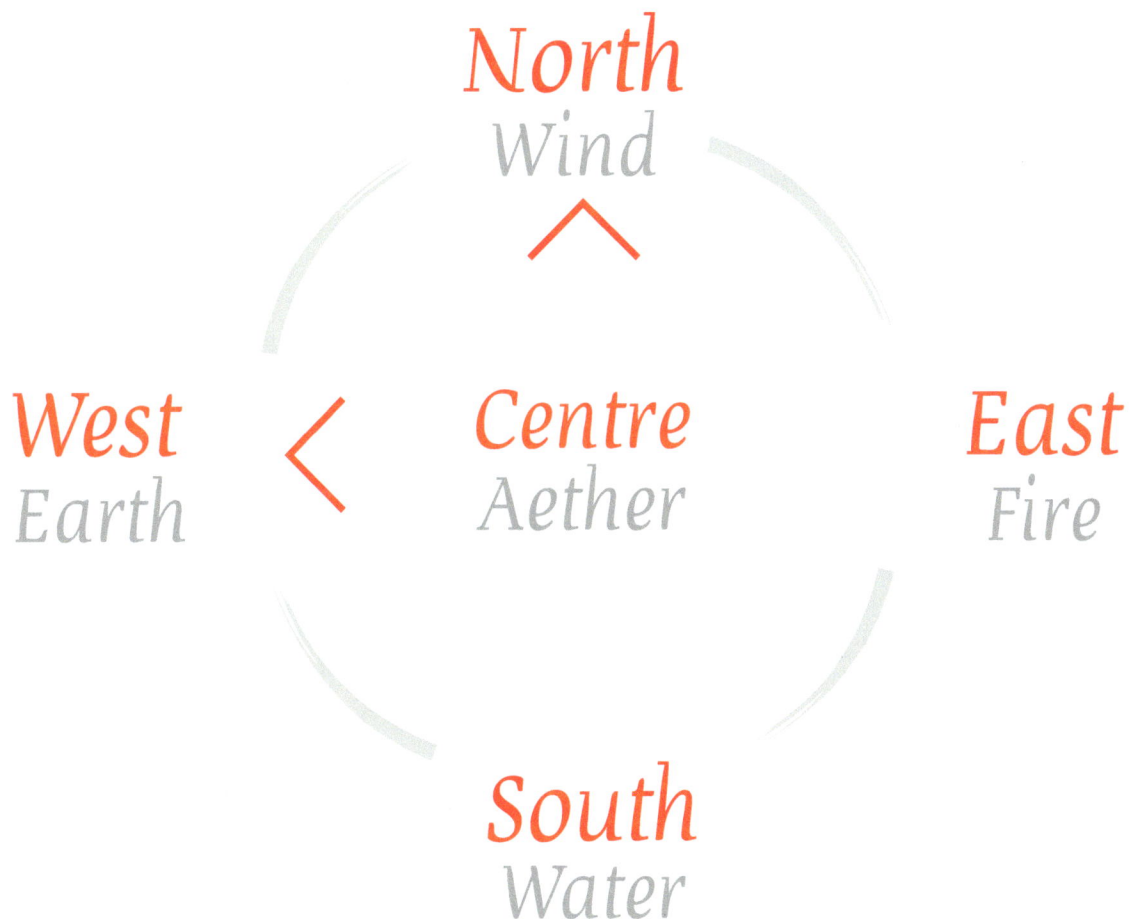

North
Wind

West
Earth

Centre
Aether

East
Fire

South
Water

The elements maintain the balance of the earth, given birth from the void in the first sound from which all life was formed.

In the East of the Wheel of elements is Fire, Grandfather Sun in the Native American tradition. The Sun that brightens the new day with each dawn and is the initiating force of our own life and fire.

In the West of the circle of elements is the earth, Grandmother Earth. A stable balanced element of holding, containing the seeds of all life. The female aspect who receives the life-giving force of the male Sun rising in the East.

The South of the circle contains the element of water which nurtures life and brings the 'Way of Beauty' in the Native American tradition. This is the place of the child born from the song of creation between the Sun and the Earth. Water brings forth the seeds of trees, plants and flowers contained within the body of the earth, the rivers, lakes and great oceans held in the Earth.

In the North is the element of air in the winds that move across the world as an unseen force defined by smoke, incense, mists and cloud, carrying the voices of the ancients, all the words that have been spoken and sung, and contain the matters of the heart. All prayers. We breathe the air into our mouths and lungs, into our hearts. The breath of life. This is the place of the adult connected to the living Earth.

Beginning in the east with the element of Fire, the movement of the circle of elements reaches across to the west, into the element of earth. The Earth-mother receives the fire within her body to quicken the seeds of life, and then moves to the South and the element of water necessary for growth. From the waters of the South, the direction moves to the North, into the element of air.

As the Sun rises in the east and sets in the west, so the direction of the circle holds the reflection of the natural world in life, death and re-birth. This is the 'nagual' energetic presence, and in the movement from South to North, of growth from child to adult, is the 'tonal', our everyday reality.

The first centre of energy is situated in the human body at the base of the spine. The Sun, as the male energy-giver, and the Earth as the female energy-receiver, meet at this point within our own body and ignite the first sphere of clear red light which begins to spin gently. This energy of fire spiralling upwards through our human physical form is as a snake rising within the body, and is the life- force awakening in the fire bringing illumination and a concentrated radiance which enlivens the bright spirit within.

The fire is the entrance of creativity. The song that is brought back from our conception which was begun in the centre of the elements. The first vibration of the aetheric centre is the soul essence coming into being. The serpent fire signifies the beginning of conscious expansion, and within this fire is contained our possibility of growth, our creative potential, and passionate expression. The snake Ouroboros biting its own tail to form a fire wheel of new possibility opening from the aetheric centre.

Awareness of our own Fire brings the experience of all Fire. The hearth that is the heart of the home, the ceremonial fires celebrating festival and sacred rites. The lightning fire and the slow-burning embers. The still small flame of a candle. Every fire contains the potential for change, as a crucible that burns away impurity, new growth follows fire.

Fire teaches us about equanimity, a balanced life-giving place of grace that burns steadily. Fire is the protector and guardian of our passionate enlivened selves and is at our beginning and at our end. Death and transformation are our unchangeable fate. We can choose to change our consciousness and to change that is to change all. The energy released at the moment of conception and the moment of death is the process of regeneration which always begins by a division, a separation. Regeneration is the transmutation of matter from opacity to radiance which is conscious and encompasses others within it, as the invisible worlds are entered.

From the central point of the circle of elements as the aetheric realm becomes manifest, as it is infused with the fire of the Sun, everything can be potentised. Aether is the place from which matter forms, an endless flow of possibilities and patterns. From the void comes the zero point of all and everything, the soul essence. The serpent fire signifies the power of conscious expansion through the higher realms, and within this fire, the first centre of energy in the human body, is contained our possibility of growth and understanding.

A Sheela-na-gig from Behy Castle, Co. Sligo, Ireland, relocated onto the wall of a stone barn. An age-old symbol of fertility, this stone carving has been painted red for many generations. It is thought to be a goddess figure holding the healing and re-generative powers of Life, Fertility and Death.

A depiction of the Mother Goddess of Lespughe, a mammoth ivory statue from about 20,000- 18,000,BC. France.

The Mineral World

The second energy centre in the body is in the west of the element wheel and is the mineral world of the Earth.

North
Gemstones

∧

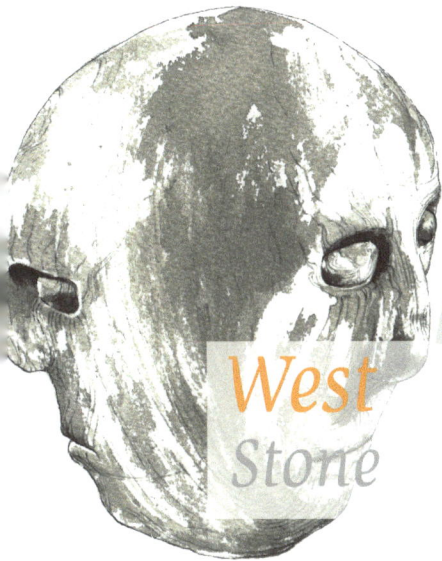

West
Stone

<

Centre
Metals~ore

East
Crystal

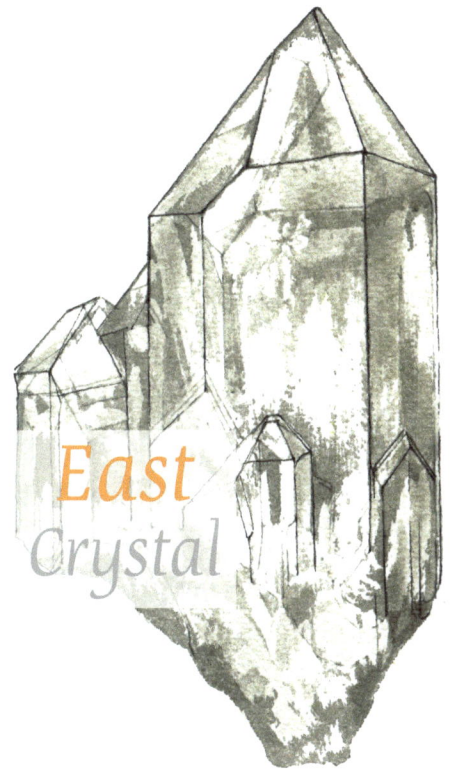

South
Sand

The second wheel of light in the body is situated in the ovaries of a woman, the womb, and the testes of the male. The Earth, Grandmother Earth is the wisdom keeper. Mother of sustenance and form, containing the sounds, pulses and songs of creation. She gives our Dream of life a vessel and within her body are the seeds of creation.

This is the 'looking within' place of intuition and initiation. The darkness illuminated by two spinning spheres of clear orange light in constant steady motion within the body. The glowing orange cave of the Earth womb from which we are born.

In the East of the mineral wheel contained by the Earth are the crystals, the memory and brain cells of the Grandmother. Transmitters of knowledge and lightning perception. The ancient beautiful structures of all that is known.

In the west is stone, the body and strength of the Grandmother. The bones of the Earth. A library of stone containing the memory of all the beginnings and transformations that have occurred and still resonate throughout the body of the Grandmother. The mountains that connect the Dreaming earth with the stars, the standing stones that speak of the First people. The patterns of origin etched into the structure of each pebble. This is the Grandmother body of knowledge and the birthing place of life.

In the South are the sands that cover the Earth, from the vast desert sandunes to the ocean floors. A constant shifting presence forming and re-forming. Imbued with the prayers of the First Nations in the healing circles and the blessings of the Tibetan people and carried by the winds and the waters.

The North holds the gemstones, the treasure of the Earth born from the energy of heat and pressure to form beings of light and substance, containing the wisdom of the Grandmother in beauty and purity of resonance.

In the centre of the mineral world are the mixed ores formed in the deep caves, the stalagmites and stalactites creating the pillars of the Earth. The living energy of the metals of gold, silver and copper which are the shining veins in the substance of the earth, and at the molten iron core of the Grandmother, the heart of the Earth, comes the song of our creation.

In the East of the mineral world, the crystal wheel can be opened into a revealing of the crystal world. Each direction of the wheel endlessly expanding like the ripples of concentric circles of water after pebbles are dropped into a still pool.

Citrine in the East, a bright, clear yellow quartz, transforms and balances, opening the first energy centre in the body into radiant light. Citrine is held by smokey quartz in the West of the crystal circle. A grounding and protective energy that clears the mind and body. Rose quartz in the South brings harmony into consciousness, calming the emotional body and opening the heart, linked to the North of the circle, where clear quartz brings focused thought and clarity. Clear quartz is the bridging energy of the physical body and the mind, and is the communicator. In the centre of the crystal circle is amethyst, a catalyst which changes lower frequencies of energy into higher levels of awareness, clearing the auric field around the body and bringing composure.

The mineral world contains the very beginning processes of the world, in the union between the Sun and the Earth, it carries the imprint of the creation of the universe within its crystalline form.

The Earth mother, venerated by the ancients, contains within her fertile body the seeds of all beginning. We live upon the body of the Earth and within the caves of crystal and stone, the first homes were provided for the people. The glowing orange cave of the Dream-bowl of the Earth and contained within the mineral structure of the world, is the divine spark of which we are a part. We are spirit enclosed in matter, a perfect reflection.

Clear Quartz

N

∧

W   <   C   >   E

Smokey Quartz   *Amethyst*   *Citrine*

S

Rose Quartz

Cast bronze statue of a
girl dancing, from Neury-
en-Sullias (Loiret), first
century AD, Musée
Historique, Orléans.

The Plant World

The third energy centre in the body is in the South of the wheel of elements and is the plant world and the waters.

North
Flowers Fruit Nuts

West
Herbs

Centre
Teacher Plants

East
Trees

South
Grasses ~ Seaweeds

The third energy centre in the human body is situated at the umbilical area from which the golden thread of life is touched by the Sun. A clear yellow triangle of light that vibrates with the energy of the world of plants and of the waters that germinate the seeds held in the Earth. This is the place of flowers, the 'way of Beauty' in the Native American tradition and the innocence of the child.

In the south of the circle of the elements, the waters of the earth move to the phases of the Moon. The great tides advancing and retreating at the edges of the vast oceans held by the earth, the source of all life. The rivers and waterfalls, the mists and rains which bring the smell of the soil and promise of growth. The sacred wells of the Celtic peoples containing the water that shows us our own reflection. In the flowing currents beneath the mirror surface of the lakes that resonate with our own watery bodies of emotional responses, and in the depths of the great seas, the memory of our becoming is held.

From the Celtic tradition comes Manannán MacLír, rider of the crested wave, the waves are his steeds and when the sea is agitated, the tresses of Manannán's wife are tossed. Lord of the Island of Emhain Abhlach, (Emhain of the apple trees), included amongst the Tuatha Dé, he leads King Cormac Mac Airt from Tara to his otherworld court. He holds the water veil of forgetfulness. God of the sea and the Otherworld.

In the East of the plant world are the trees, rooted in the Earth, their branches stretching to the Sun and the Moon. The forests, jungles and woodlands breathing with the tides, providing food and shelter, they hold the patterns of the seasons in the rings of their bodies. In this place are the sacred Celtic languages of the trees. The ash tree, fuinseóg, venerated above all trees in Irish Celtic antiquity, the five greatest trees of Ireland were magical ash trees used to make warriors' spears, its association with life and death still acknowledged as a funerary tree with prayers and offerings. The Sacred Trees, 'bile' were named Tree of Tortu, Oak of Maghna, Yew of Ross, Bough of Daithi and Ash of Uisneach. The Tree of Life, Crann Beithe, of the great Celtic tribes who named themselves 'men of the tree 'Fir Bile'.

In the West of the plant wheel are the herbs and healing plants whose energy leans towards us to give the essence of their being as medicine and food. The plants teach of the give-away and from their world comes the healing sleep of regeneration, and the enlivening of the sense of taste in the food we eat. The ancient art of the herbalist gives medicine to the people.

In the South are the grasses on the great plains of the Earth, moving in the winds, providing grain and rice. The sedges and reeds of the marshlands give shelter in thatched roofs and cloth made from flax. In the oceans are the seaweeds flowing in the currents, the underwater grasses.

In the North are the sweet foods of fruits, nuts and berries and the flowers with the yellow pollen clustered in their centres, a reflection of the Sun. The refined and scented essence of beauty.

At the centre of the plant circle are the teacher plants. These are the plants that contain potent energies revered by the first people of Earth for the teachings and strength they bring to the mind and spirit. They are the Ayahuasca vine, the sacred mushrooms, the peyote cactus, that bring visions and healing to the people, revealing the plant consciousness. These plants are approached with reverence and honouring in the sacred traditions. Here also is the white sage and tobacco plant of the Native American cleansing and blessing way. The spirit of the plants, Quetzal, the embodiment of Beauty.

Stone carving of triple spiral, Newgrange chamber, central recess. Neolithic monument 3,200 BC, Co. Meath, Ireland.

A scene from one of the outer plates of the Gundestrup cauldron showing a deity holding a stag in each hand.

The Animal World

The fourth centre of energy in the body is in the north of the wheel of elements and encompasses the world of animals.

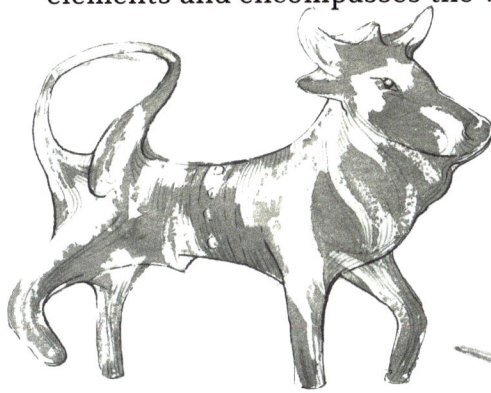

North
four legged

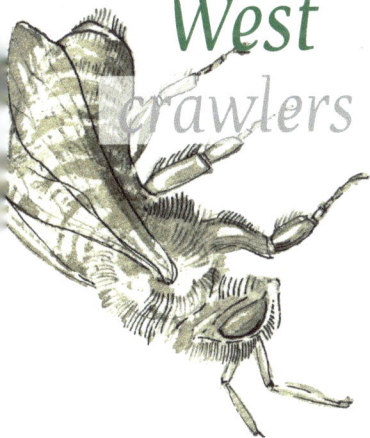

West
crawlers

Centre
mythical~ human

East
winged

South
swimmers

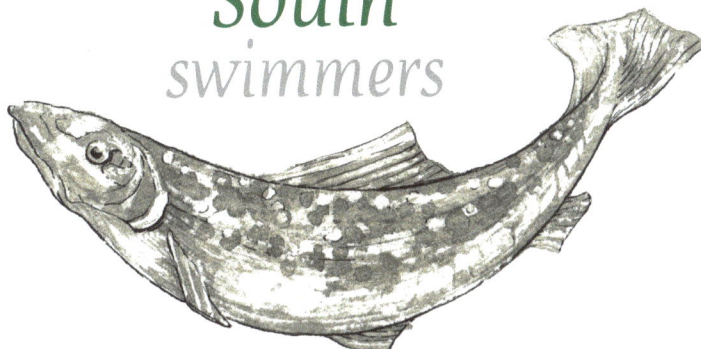

The fourth wheel of light is situated in the heart. A clear emerald green star, gently spinning. This is the place of the adult who stands with heart in the world connected to the living Earth. In this place, Coatl, the spirit of all animals and the embodiment of heart teaches us of the animal world, second born of the Earth.

In the East are the birds, the winged ones, teachers of flight. They are the dawn chorus greeting the rising of the Sun with their songs that pierce the unconscious mind and awaken us into light. They are protector of the egg from which all life emerges. Masters of the elements of air, vibrating in resonance with the winds. All-seeing bright eyes, they navigate the streams of warm and cool air that rise and fall across the lands and the sea.

In the West are the crawling animals and the insects. The bees that pollinate the flowers and plants. In the shining wings of beetles, and the iridescent bodies of the damselflies and dragonflies is the reflection of the Dream of beauty. The many-coloured butterflies, counted as the souls of fallen warriors in the Celtic tradition, teach of transformation. Here, also are the snakes containing the mystery of venom, their bodies close to the earth, attuned to each strand, each direction in the web of life.

In the South are the swimmers. The great whales, dreamers of the sea, who sing beneath the waters of the ancient memory of land and the deep mystery of the ocean. The dolphins skimming the waves with joy. Silvery fish shoals turning as one in the changes of the currents. The seals, keening on the rocks at the shores, calling the selkie home, and the salmons' fertile journey to the spawning pools, leaping waterfalls to find their way to the clear cold waters of beginning and end.

In the North are the four-legged animals, who walk and run upon the Earth, living a perfect-balanced knife-edge of life and death, in watchful awareness. From the great herds who follow the migratory pathways across the land, and the predatory packs who hunt them, to the smallest animal collecting seeds to feed its young. The animals carry on their fur and skin the markings and colours of the living Earth. The stag standing in the forest, the heart of the land.

In the centre of the circle are the mythological animals, the dragon, emblem of Wales, and the wild land of the Celts and the old religion. Guardian of the mysteries, elemental quicksilver. The feathered serpent of the Mayan tradition, encircling the Earth as a rainbow of fire, water and air. The Viking dragon ships protecting the warriors and the immortal dragons of China. In the centre is the endless renewal of the phoenix rising from the fire purifying and transforming energy, and the griffin of air and earth, born from the sun, protector of innocence. The mythological animals, known in every culture, emanate from the aetheric realms, carrying the knowledge contained in the elements that have formed the world.

Animal/shaman dancing. Les Trios Freres cave, Ariege, France. 14,000 BC.

Cernunnos, the horned god of Celtic tradition who bears the horns of the stag, ram or bull upon his head, is Lord of the animals, protector and ruler of his realm, keeper of the forest and summoner of all animals and serpents with his stag roar. The Kingly Bull, Stag god and master of the magical boar who leads its hunters to the otherworld. Flidhais, goddess of the forest animals and wild deer, accompanied by birds, who becomes a swan and in her other form, she is Badbh, the hooded crow.

The Otherworld is the Celtic dream of fluidity between the natural and supernatural worlds which constantly shift from animal to mortal form, changing into the animals, birds, fish and insects of the animal realm, which were painted and tattooed onto the bodies of Celtic warriors so that they could join the Wildhunt that leads to the Otherworld where time is changed and transformation takes place.

The animal wheel teaches of balance within the movement of life, they teach of courage and heart, and of guardianship and protection of family and group, to hold and nurture the future generation. They are our family on this earth. In the North, the place of receiving in the circle, it is possible to understand the interconnected relationship between the human world and the animals as heart wisdom is opened with the breath of life.

Bronze figure with enamelled eyes from Bouray (Seine et Oise) wearing a torc around its neck and sitting in a 'yoga' posture associated with deity figures. Musée des Antiquités Nationales, St. Germain-en-Laye, France. Dated 3rd century BC.

The Human World

The human world is in the centre of the circle. The fifth energy wheel in the human body is at the throat. The clear blue five-pointed star of the Sacred Human.

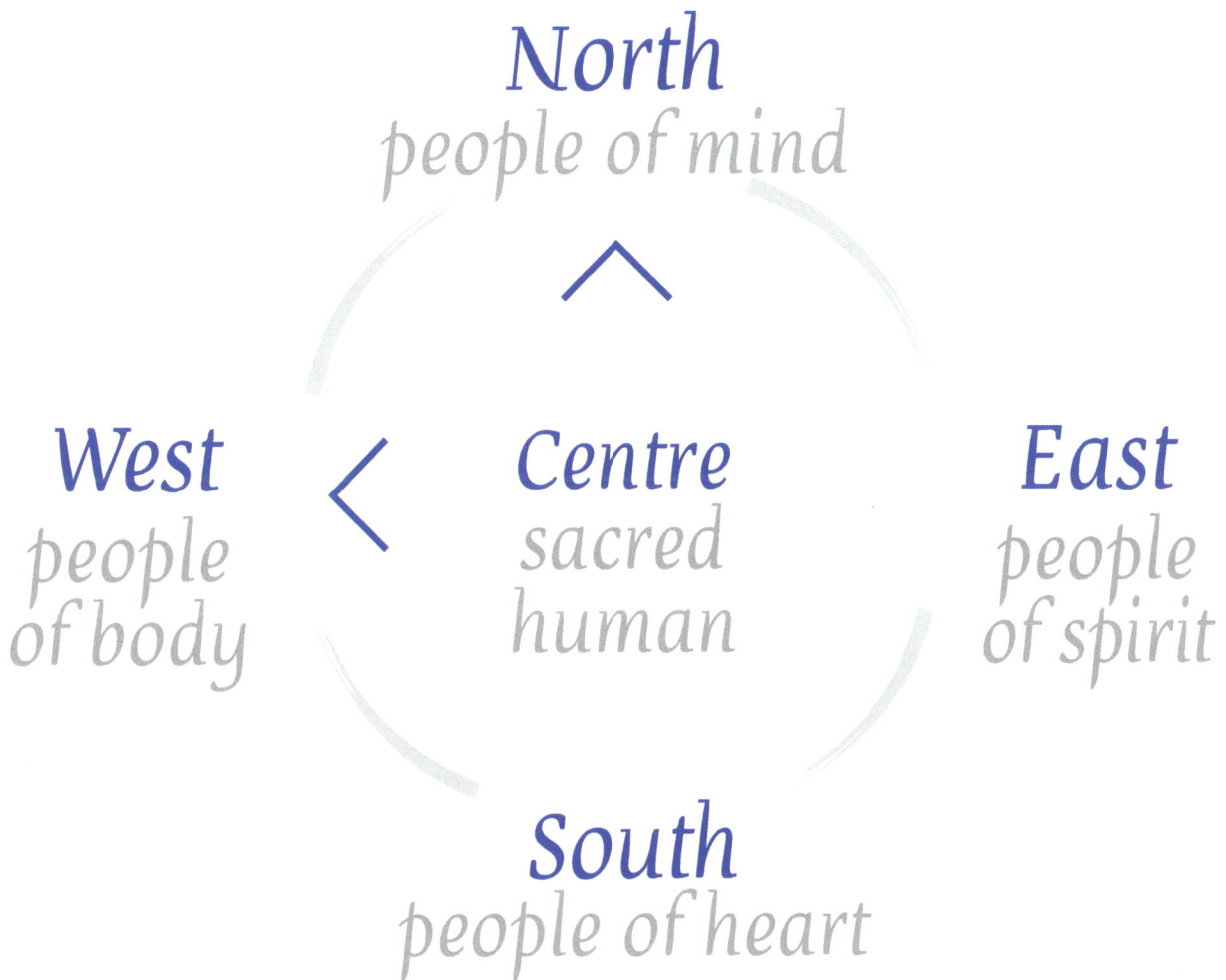

North
people of mind

West
people of body

Centre
sacred human

East
people of spirit

South
people of heart

In the East of the human world are the people of spirit. The lineage holders of the great religious traditions of the world, dedicating their lives within that tradition. Contained within the mysteries of every religion lie the seeds of enlightenment and growth.

In the West are the people of body with the knowledge of healing and of the deep resonances and rhythms of the human body in connection to the Earth. In this place are the dancers and athletes.

In the South are the people of heart, containing compassion and understanding, the awareness of others in empathy and the protectors of the family and tradition, called the 'red road' by the First peoples of the Americas.

In the North are the people of mind, those whose ideas and intellectual accomplishments have enhanced our lives in medicine, technology and inventiveness. The philosophers and thinkers.

In the centre of the circle is the Sacred Human balanced in mind, body and spirit.

The human world is a celebration of life in connection to the Earth, and to all others who are a reflection of self. In this place is the expansion of the variety of the people who inhabit the world, their different religions, customs and culture, with their collective impulse to go forwards in the new generations of children. The Sacred Law that 'nothing shall be done that harms the child' shows us how to live in a shared provision uniting the human world with the other worlds contained by the Earth. As human determiners we are able to make decisions with discernment and courage, bringing the heart-strength of the animal world, the generosity of the plant world and the stability of the mineral world.

The sacred Human, balanced between the worlds of the Earth, brings the music of songs and stories to the people, drawing on the culture and wisdom of all the races to give to the children in the world they inherit.

The Flowering Tree ceremony from the Native American tradition is a profound teaching of our true nature. Designed to show us our heart, it is required within the tradition to be undertaken many times. The questions are asked at the foot of a flowering tree in each direction, starting in the South, at the place of the child. Finding our own voice, our own expression, our own song of life to become a bridge between spirit and substance.

Why am I here?   Where do I come from?   Where am I going?   Who am I?

The Bardic tradition from the Celtic people celebrates the voice that carries the wisdom and memory of the people in the music and songs that could enchant or satirise. The bards were lawkeepers, holding the balance of accountability within

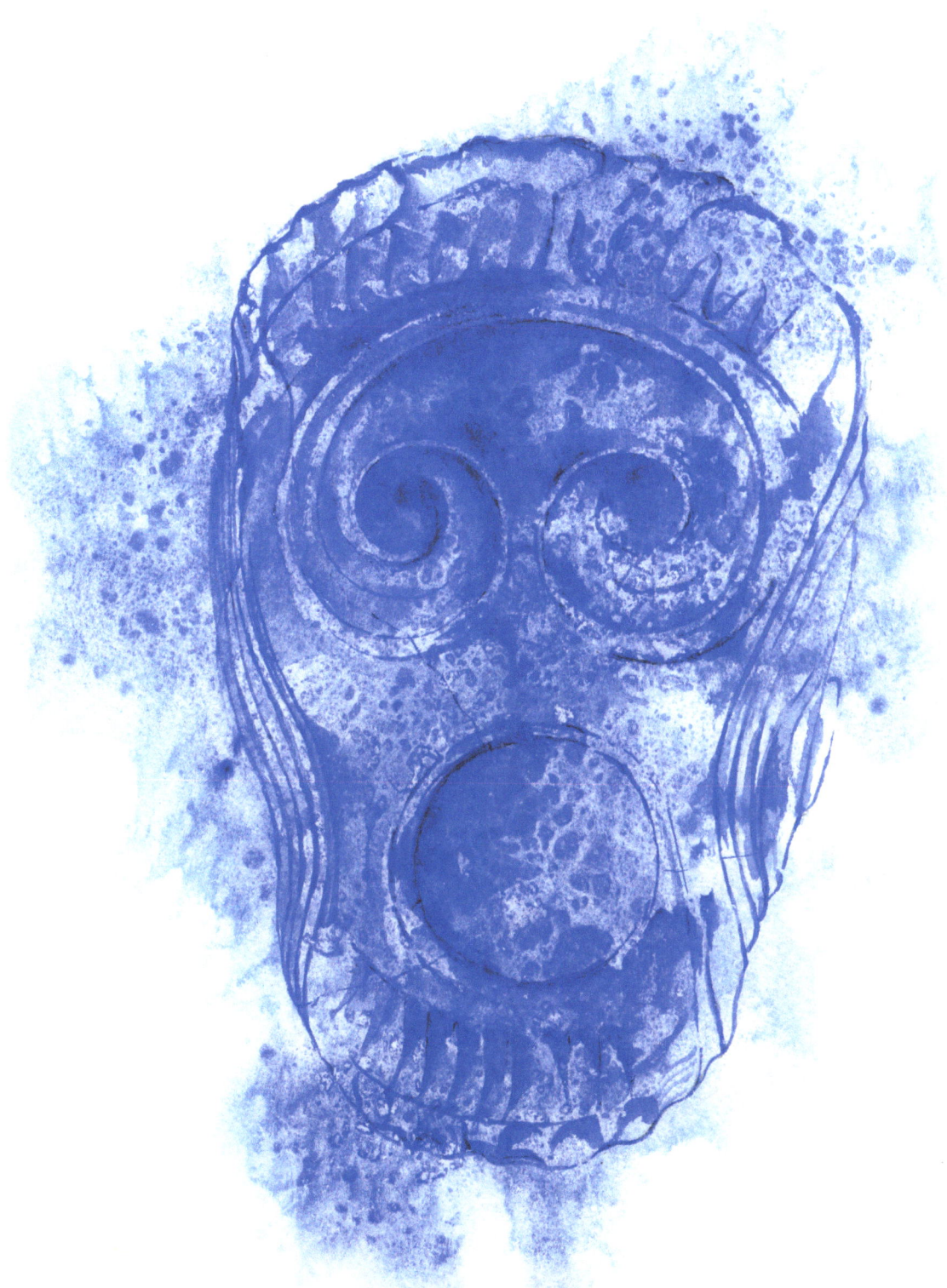

Head made of polished flint. Found in the east tomb of Knowth, Boyne Valley, Co. Meath, Ireland. Dated from 3,500 – 3,200 BC.

the knowledge of the old ways of being, in the singing of the lineages, keepers of memory and composers of the present.

In the centre of the circle, the aetheric limitless space contains the beginning of all creation from which the humans, the two-legged have emerged surrounded by the worlds of mineral, plant and animal life held by the body of the earth, to make possible a vision of the future where inspiration and creativity in thought and action becomes actualised in the form of the sacred Human, touched by the divine and connected to all living beings.

Bronze mask from
Garancieres-en-Beance.
Musée des Beaux Arts,
Chartes, France. From
around the 4th century BC.

The Ancestral World

The sixth energy centre in the human body is in the forehead, at the place of the third eye. A clear amethyst six-pointed star.

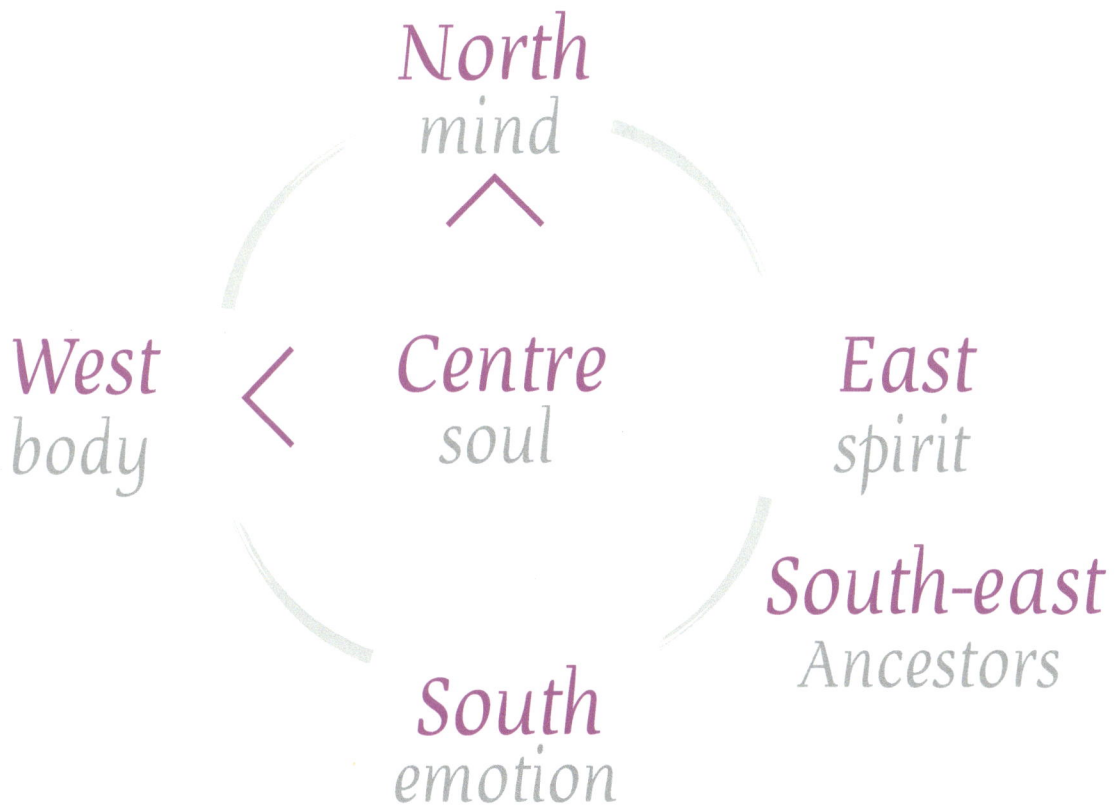

North
mind

West
body

Centre
soul

East
spirit

South-east
Ancestors

South
emotion

The ancestors are placed in the South-East of the directional wheel. It is here that the opening is made available to our blood ancestors who brought us our life, and have gone before us with their experience and the knowledge gained from their life-times that resonate within our own bodies. A pattern of remembering in the cells, a mirror of reflection within. From the First People who lived and left their paintings and hand-prints in the caves of the earth, to the people of the modern world, the connection to the past is carried in the cells of our being. The countless generations who have gone before us have left the imprint of their lives in our bodies.

The sixth energy centre, the third eye, opens to allow us to see clearly and becomes a conduit for the wisdom of the ancients to be known and understood. Living with the awareness of those who have gone before gives meaning to our actions. The sixth centre of light perceives directly, knows instantly, sees clearly without judgement from the mind.

At the South-East of the circle are the Earth guardians, the spirits of the Earth known as the Toliliquai in the Native American traditions, the Shining Ones and the Little People in the Celtic tradition. Everything in this world is alive, each rock, each flower and tree, the rivers and oceans, all have consciousness and this is expressed and guarded by the spirits. Some are large, like the spirit of a mountain, and some are small, and life vibrates within and around them. The seers' eye in the sixth energy centre knows this.

Images from the rock art of the Spanish Levant Mesolithic age.

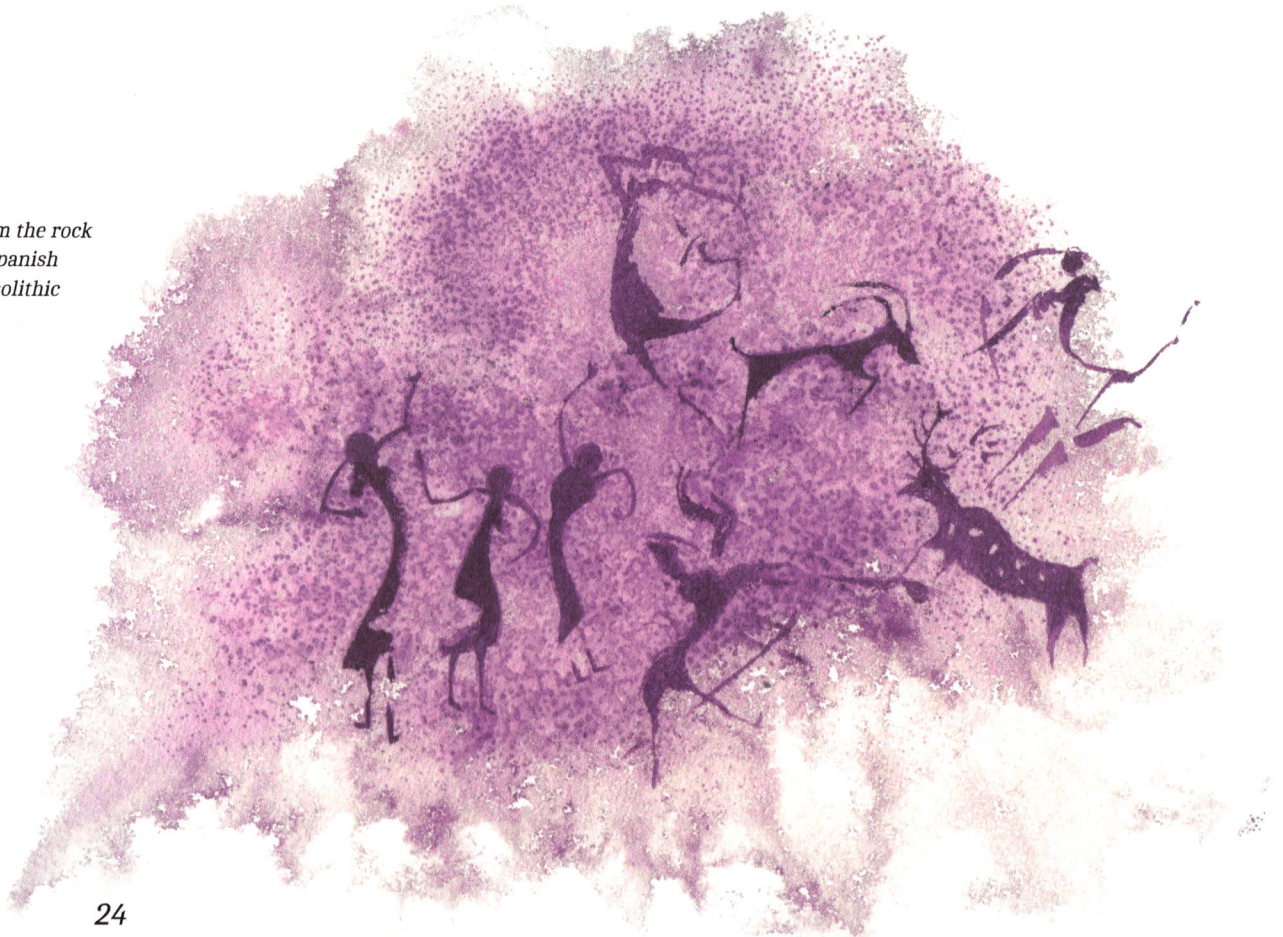

A scene from one of the outside plates of the Gundestrup Cauldron showing a goddess figure with two smaller figures behind of a male and a female.

Knowledge of the ancestral lineage can be remembered with the **Ceremony of the Ancients**. At the left shoulder and streaming behind us are the maternal lineages, at the right shoulder are the paternal lineages. The Dream of our becoming can be known for seven generations before our birth as we fall back into the awareness of all those who have gone before and feel the vibrational essence of the ancestors who stand behind us and who walk with us in life.

The third eye perceives the beauty and mystery of the world, penetrating the layers of illusion to arrive at the luminous core of truth, bringing the wisdom of the ancients to the fore and into the present to see the shining web of life that surrounds us.

Wrought-iron mask of a deity from Alencon (Maine-et-Loire). Musée St. Jean, Angers, France.

The Dream

The seventh energy centre in the body is at the top of the head and is the seven-pointed star of clear violet light, the Dreamwheel.

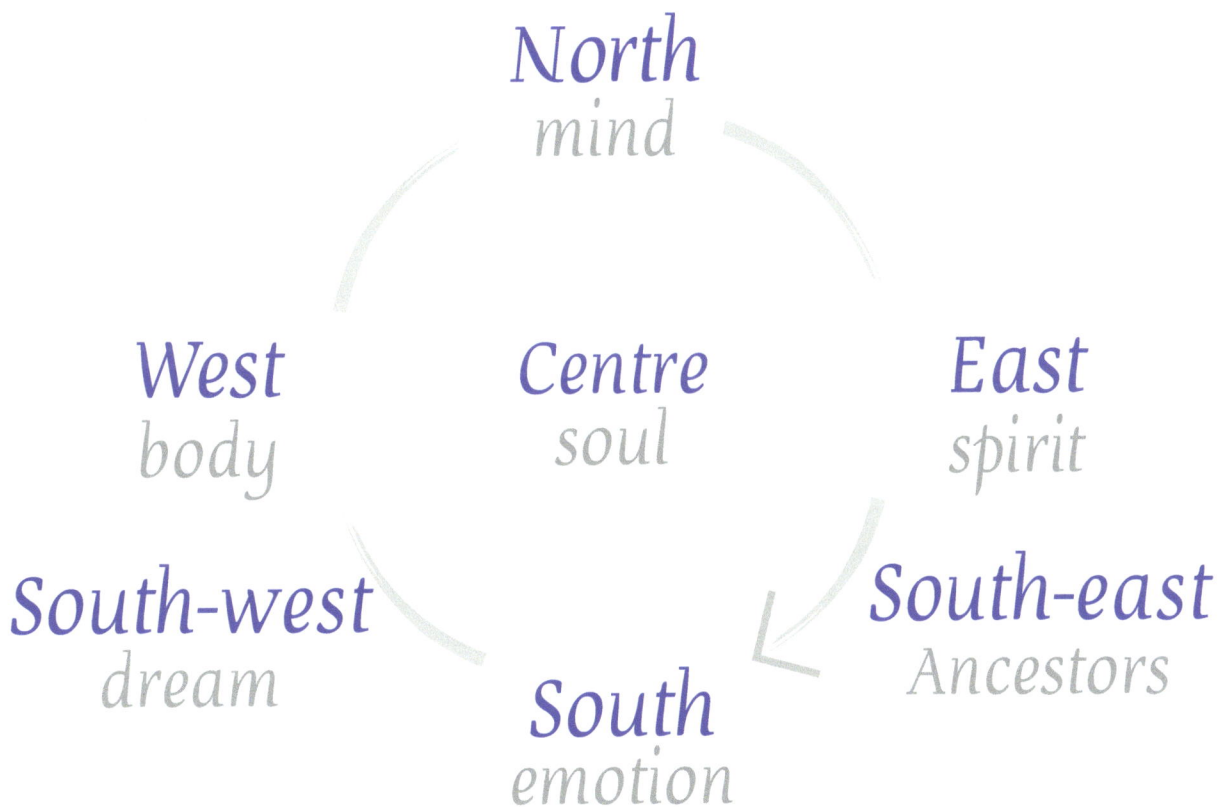

North
mind

West
body

Centre
soul

East
spirit

South-west
dream

South
emotion

South-east
Ancestors

Silver horse
ornament with head
trophies around a
central solar boss,
4th-2nd century BC.

The Dream is in the South-West of the directional circle and is life itself. It is how we are in life, our passion and involvement with life and it is the Dream of the Earth and her worlds. It is the Dream of life lived with heart, our Sacred Dream which can enter the collective Dream for the good of all.

The Wheel of Dreams is the violet crown at the top of the head bringing the visionary Dream of the enlightened Sacred Human into consciousness for all of the worlds of the Earth, and it is the opening that connects each human life to its divine origin.

The Dreamwheel is the place from which we leave our individual concerns to enter the wider consciousness of all life, and it is the entry point where understanding is received. Each human child is born with the soft spot at the top of the head, the fontanelle, open and permeable, living the first few weeks of life completely in the Dream. The Hopis say that the sacred Human walks the ways of the world with the top of the head open, connected to all life in the world and all Dreaming consciousness.

In the Celtic tradition the heads of fallen warriors were venerated and preserved. These severed heads were put in cavities in doorposts and lintels so that they could speak to the living of truth and prophesy. The head, as a sacred vessel, contained the wisdom and knowledge of the future and protected the Dream of the people. All spiritual matters were held within the head.

Everything is a Dream and each person can choose the Dream that they wish to live within. The Dream can be a complete awareness of a sacred way of being where the unconscious is revealed. Awakening within the Dream to become conscious is a discipline that requires sobriety. Every thought, every word, every action affects other living beings on the earth and in this life-dance we need to find our Dream, our purpose of being, and to enter into it fully to fulfil our own lives and to create a world of beauty for the future generations.

Bronze mask from South Cadbury, Somerset. Mid 1st century AD, UK.

Figure of a Celtic warrior. Bronze. Dated from the first to second century BC.

Cycles & Patterns

The eighth energy centre is the octagonal black star surrounding
and defining the physical body.

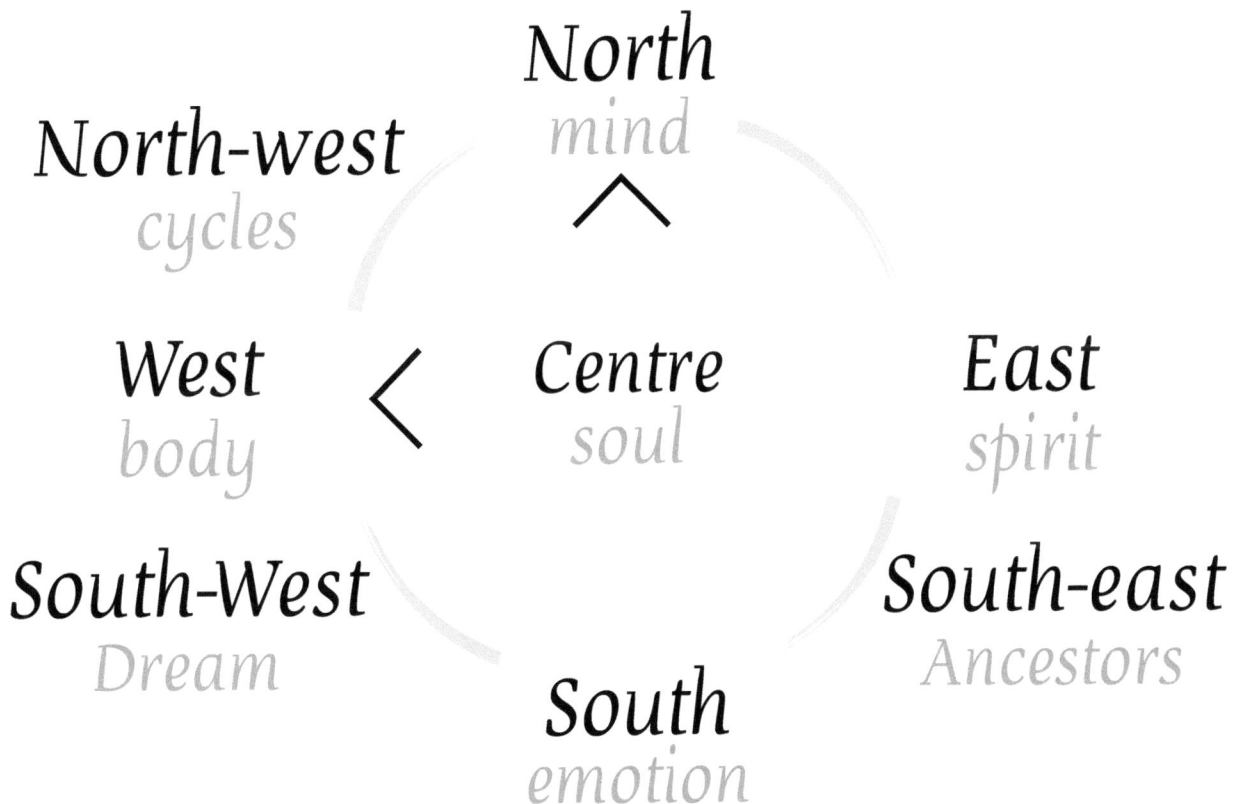

North
mind

North-west
cycles

West
body

Centre
soul

East
spirit

South-West
Dream

South-east
Ancestors

South
emotion

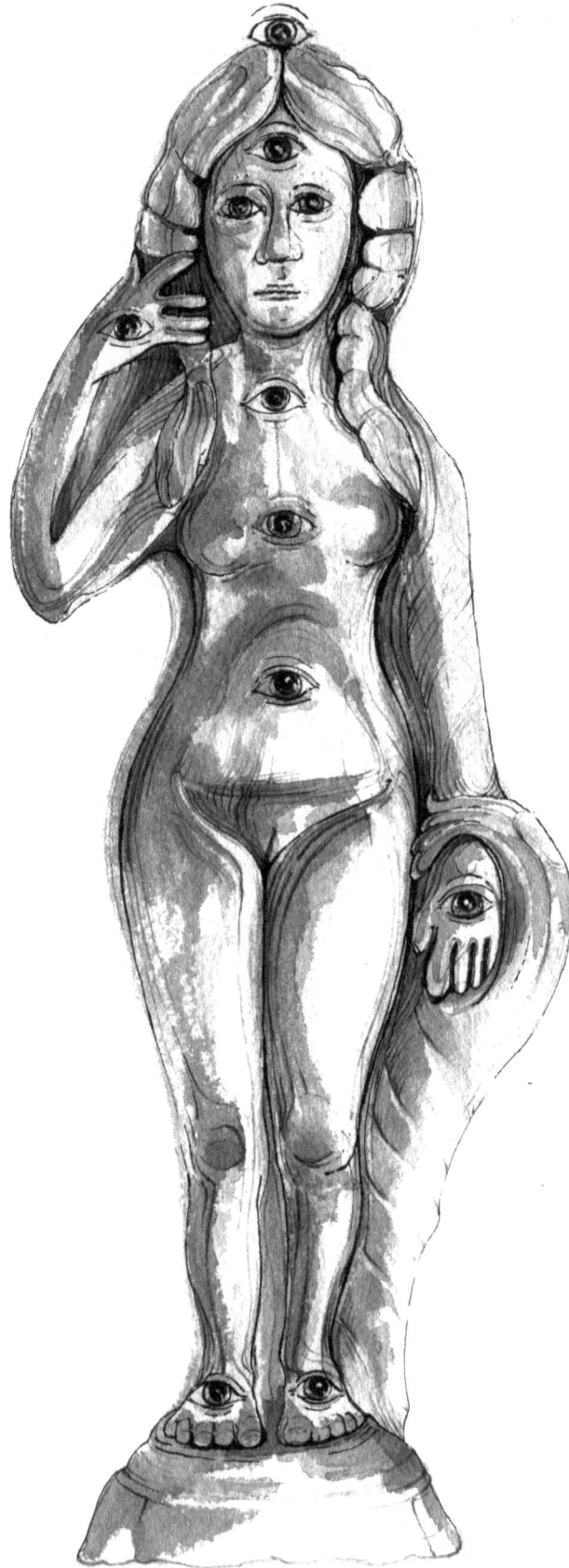

*Clay figure of a Celtic
goddess, 1st-2nd century
AD, Museum of London.*

In the North-West of the directional circle are the cycles and patterns locked within our bodies in this life-time. The North-West is the place of rules and laws, and there is an opportunity for transformation through Sacred Law.

The human body fired by the energy of the Sun, held by the solidity of the Earth, connected to all forms of life, and open to the consciousness of the Dream, can move to a level of awareness and refinement of understanding that transforms every cell in the body. The pattern of life is understood and repeating cycles that spiral through the existence of each individual, are released. The human body can be transformed, the mind cleared and a true focus in life can be obtained. The ten eyes are opened and the five ears are opened.

The left eye is the subjective eye

The right eye sees objective reality

The third eye in the centre of the forehead sees all reality both past and present, and the world of spirit.

The fourth eye is the male animal eye at the back of the neck and the heart female eye, and sees truth and untruth, and danger.

The fifth eye at the top of the head is the Dream eye and sees into the Dream and memory.

The sixth eye is in the palm of the left hand and sees spirit emanations.

The seventh eye is in the palm of the right hand and sees Dream emanations.

The eighth eye is in the sole of the left foot and sees the patterns of the past.

The ninth eye is in the sole of the right foot and sees the design of energy.

The tenth eye is in the belly button and sees the totality (soul essence) of all things.

The five ears are opened;

The left ear is opened for subjective hearing

The right ear is opened for objective hearing

The third ear inside the head hears all the voices of our inner dialogue

The fourth ear at the heart hears all truth, and all that is not spoken

The fifth ear at the belly button hears all and everything, all songs, all messages and hears the voice of Great Spirit

The third eye and the third ear can read all

Our bodies are connected to the worlds of the earth, to the minerals, plants and animals. We are not separate, but a part of the living Earth, as the earth is part of us.

Life is a dance upon the Earth and living our life in Sacred Law which honours the Earth and her worlds, we can obtain freedom from the patterns and cycles repeating within ourselves. The way through the knot can be seen and the sacred thread of life can be followed into light.

Focus and intent, like the spear thrown by the Celtic warriors or the arrow shot by the Native American soldier can pierce the mist of forgetfulness and confusion to form a clear pathway forward that aligns the human with the worlds of the Earth. Living a life of conscious action, informed by an honouring and awareness of all life creates balance and harmony, called 'The Beauty Way' by the First People of the Americas.

The human body given to each one of us to be tested, challenged, understood and enjoyed is our vehicle upon the Earth. The eight-pointed star of black light contains all the colours of the earth and is our arena of transformation, the warrior task we are each given to undertake in our lives.

*Spear found in river
Thames, London. Iron
with bronze overlay.
Late 1st century BC.
British Museum,
London, UK.*

Design of Energy

The ninth wheel of light in the human body is the rainbow-coloured nine pointed star of the auric field, situated just above the head and surrounding the body.

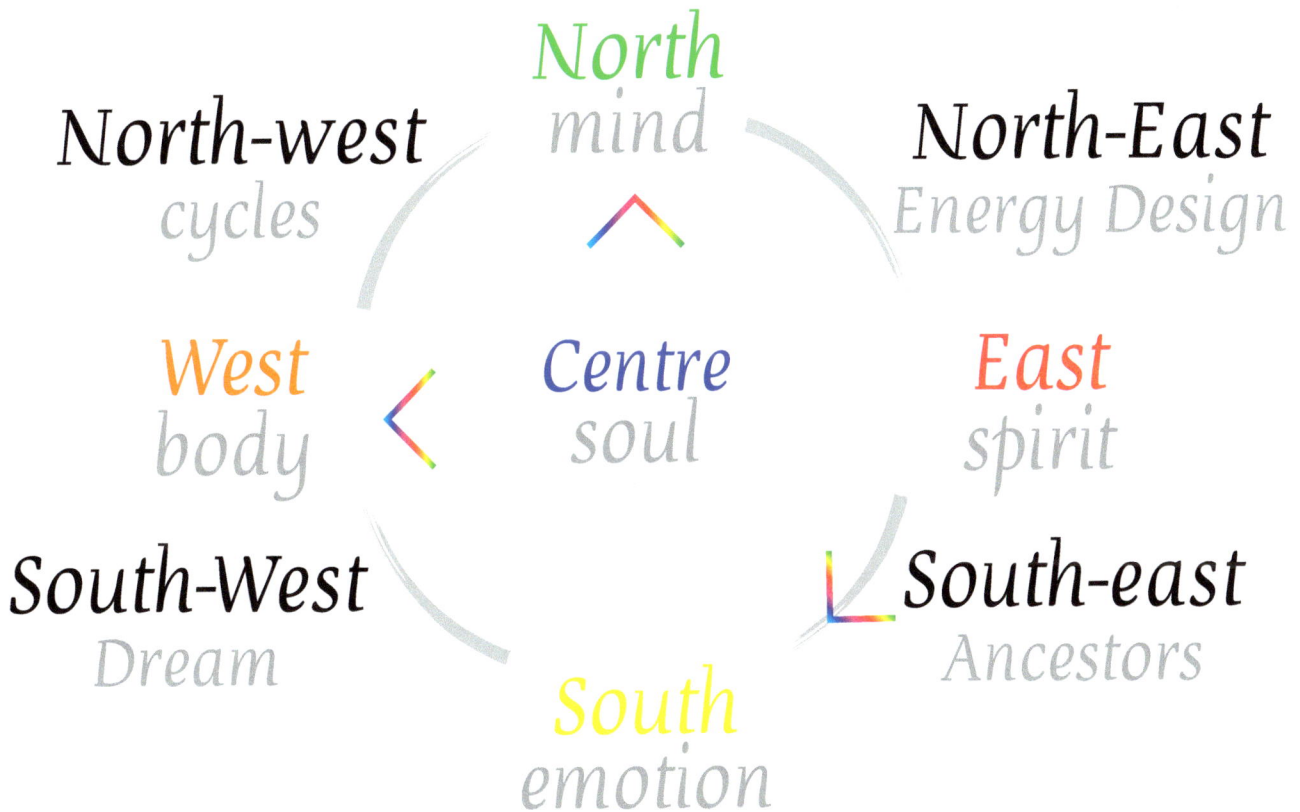

North-west
cycles

North
mind

North-East
Energy Design

West
body

Centre
soul

East
spirit

South-West
Dream

South
emotion

South-east
Ancestors

The North-East is the balance between masculine and feminine, giving and receiving, active and passive. It is the place of the design of energy in this dance of life.

As we navigate our way through this life it is possible to design our energy so that we move forwards holding a perfect balance between control and surrender, aware of the natural cycles and rhythms within the body and all that is around us, and how we interact with the world.

The nine-pointed rainbow fire of the aura is a sensory field around the body connected to the web of life held by the earth, and contains the balance of what is given and what is taken, how much that is consumed and how much that is produced. The protective field of the aura is our energetic resonance in the world and contains our patterns and experience from many lifetimes.

Amergin arrived on the ninth wave of the sea in his ship in the Celtic tradition and as he set his right foot upon the land, he saw the energy pathways of Ireland that lay before him and his people. The eyes and ears of the body protected by the field of rainbow light contained in the aura carry the possibility of enlightenment and the ability to see the Dream of ourselves and of all others, and to call upon the memory of all life-times. The ability to re-align the energy body and to change shape and become another form of life, is recalled. The eternal cycle of the natural world is known and held within the Celtic tradition as the timeless realms within the land, in the mounds and mountains of the Sídhe, and beneath the waves in the Kingdom of Manamán Mac Lír, and the mysterious Western Isles of the Tuatha de Danann.

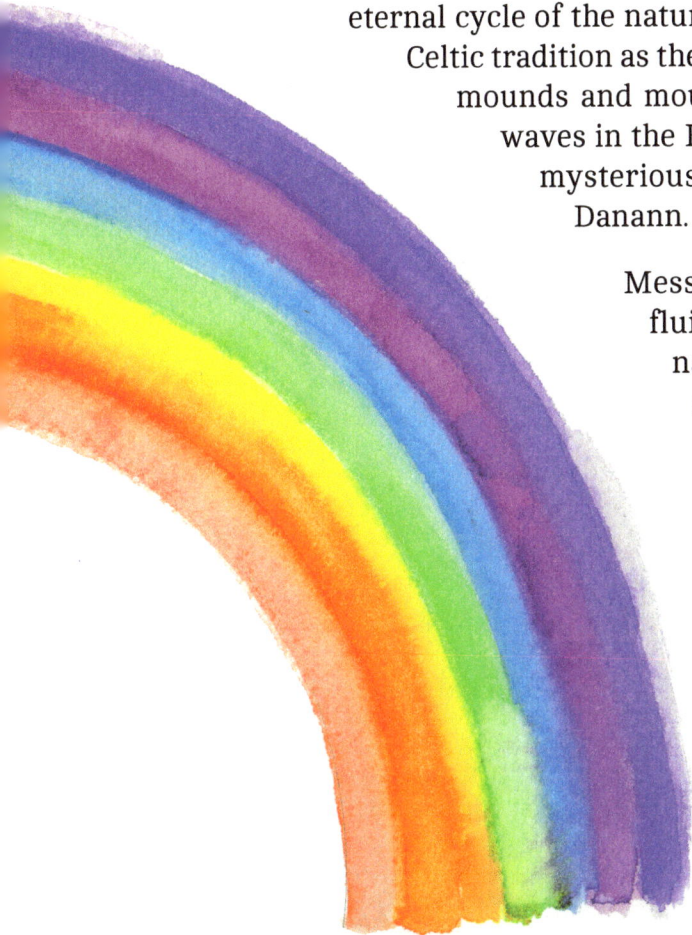

Messengers from the Otherworld move fluidly between the gateways dividing the natural world from the Otherworld, shape-shifting to blend the natural and supernatural. The auric field is the energy dancer, the ninth wave of energy contained within and around the human body, the great light wheel.

The Celtic god Lugh, Lord of Light, god of skill, skilled in all nine arts and guide of all journeys whose name means 'the Shining One' is the divine king. The harvest festival of Lughnasadh is named after him. Lugh of the Long Arm 'Lámhfhada', who stretches out his hand to the Sun and the Moon is master of the energetic body.

The North-East which completes the directions of the circle encompasses the aspects of all the directions. It contains the elements, the connection to all the worlds of the earth, the ancestors and dream, holding all in balance within the body and the aura of the human.

Brass statue found under
a tree in Co. Roscommon,
in Museum of Trinity
College, Dublin, Ireland.

All Mind - One Mind

The ten-pointed white-gold star above the head is the centre of all mind, one mind. The golden halo.

The ten pointed star of wisdom contains all that is known and all that is sacred. It is the collective consciousness of all sentient beings in the sacred wheel of life. The tenth centre of light is the universal conscious mind, the Great Sleeper Dreamer Dancer, the Ancestor Spirit dancer and the Shadow Fire Dancer. It is the golden white halo which is the soul wheel of our life force and possibility. 'As I know myself, I know all others'. The Celtic god Taranis holds the golden wheel of all seasons and the spiral which is the lightning flash of inspiration.

The spiral is a reflection of the living world around us in the shells, plants and creatures that share this world. Honoured by the Celts, the spiral is seen in the megalithic stone carvings and metal work of brooches and weaponry, to the Book of Kells illuminated by the early Christian monks in the monastic buildings of the Middle Ages. The spiral reveals the ebb and flow of eternal life and the endless cycle of birth and death. In its centre is contained the still point of all possibility turning into movement. The energy held within the human body moves in a spiralling current linking the subtle forces that connect us to the worlds of the Earth. The spiral is the language and energetic expression of the thread of life, a reflection of the spiralling galaxy of stars from which the Earth was born.

The twisted hairs society of wise elders and wisdom keepers from the Native American tradition bring together the knowledge and understanding from the different tribes to be shared and known by all. The braided hair on the stone carvings of the Celtic peoples, on the sheela-na-gigs, and the bearded figures of manuscript illumination, show the importance of the wisdom keepers in the Celtic tradition. The enlightened human of the tenth energy centre embodies the balance of spirit and heart and 'rófheassa', great knowledge exemplified in the Druid of the Celtic peoples. The braided hair and beard represent the three-fold tradition of Bard, Filidh and Druid combined in the sacred triad. The Druids were associated with Uisneach, the navel of Ireland, the place of the central fire and site of the great assembly.

The igniting energy of the Fire rises through the body, spiralling through the wheels of light that connect the human with all the living worlds of the Earth, and as the energy rises like a snake uncoiling, the human is enlivened. The tree of life unfolds around the body, and touches the numinous, Great Spirit, the Divine. The tenth centre of energy and the wisdom held in the golden white light above the head is brought gently to the beginning point, at the centre of the red flame, the igniting spark. The rainbow auric field of the ninth is joined with the second centre of glowing orange light which holds the design of energy in balance with the mineral world of the Earth. The wheel of the eight containing the patterns of this life-dance is brought to the third centre into the place of the give-away and the flowering of beauty. The violet Dream-wheel meets the emerald green star where the animal world brings balance and heart. The amethyst flame of the six-pointed star that connects the ancestors with this life is brought to the shining blue star of the Sacred Human. The luminous and completed energy body is created.

The enlightened one is at the centre of all circles, bringing the energy of change held in balance, alive in the world, connected to all that is created and containing the Divine spark, Great Spirit, which is the light and radiance of the source of being.

Celtic knotwork in the continuous line, interlacing and serpentine, symbolises the journey of life, sometimes fluid and sometimes constricted and difficult to see. The ancient Celts found expression for their understanding of the eternal movement of life in the knotwork that are keys to the patterns contained within ourselves.

The teachings of the rainbow body of light given in this book have been known and passed down to successive generations through the ages in the oral tradition of the Native American since the first times. In our modern world we increasingly live apart from our families and our countries of origin, and we see our languages and cultures fragmenting, disconnected from ourselves and each other, but we are not separate beings. We are one expression of the family of life on this Earth in relationship to all that is around us.

The teachings contained within the wheels of light are luminous as the delicate powder that falls from a moth's wing in the evening and bright as the morning light that opens our eyes and senses to the new day.

"*Every part of this earth is sacred to my people. Every shining pine needle, every sandy shore, every mist in the dark woods, every meadow, every humming insect. All are holy in the memory and experience of my people. We know the sap which courses through the trees as we know the blood that courses through our veins. We are part of the earth and it is part of us. The perfumed flowers are our sisters. The bear, the deer, the great eagle, are our brothers. The rocky crests, the juices in the meadow, the body heat of the pony, and man, all belong to the same family. The shining water that moves in the streams and rivers is not just water, but the blood of our ancestors. Each ghostly reflection in the clear water of the lakes tells us of events and memories in the life of my people. The water's murmur is the voice of my father's father. The rivers are our brothers. They quench our thirst. They carry our canoes and feed our children. So you must give to the rivers the kindness you would give to any brother. Remember that the air is precious to us, that the air shares its spirit with all the life it supports. The wind that gave our grandfather his first breath also receives his last sigh. The wind also gives our children the spirit of life... Will you teach your children what we have taught our children? That the earth is our mother. What befalls the earth, befalls all the sons of the earth. This we know; the earth does not belong to man, man belongs to the earth. All things are connected like the blood which unites all. Man did not weave the web of life, He is merely a strand in it. Whatever he does to the web, he does to himself.*"

Chief Seattle, 1855

Acknowledgements

Bain, George. Celtic Art; the methods of construction. Constable, London, 1977.

MacCana, Prionsias. Celtic Mythology. Hamlyn Publishing group Ltd, New York, 1970.

MacCulloch, J. A. The Religion of the Ancient Celts. Dover Publications, 2012.

Rees, Alywn & Rees, Brinley. Celtic Heritage, Ancient Tradition in Ireland and Wales. Thames and Hudson, 1961.

Epona, the Horse Goddess holding a torc, Alise-Ste-Reine, Burgundy, 1st-2nd century AD. Stone

www.ingramcontent.com/pod-product-compliance
Lightning Source LLC
LaVergne TN
LVHW072104070426
835508LV00003B/257